DON'T THINK: LOOK

DON'T THINK: LOOK

William Corbett

30 May '97
For Kristin + Jake —
when you put down
the chain saw
and pick something
up let it be
this book — Best,
Bill

ZOLAND BOOKS
Cambridge, Massachusetts

First edition published in 1991 by
Zoland Books, Inc.
384 Huron Avenue
Cambridge, Massachusetts 02138

Copyright © 1991 by William Corbett

All rights reserved. No part of this book may be used or reproduced in any manner whatsoever without written permission, except in the case of brief quotations embodied in critical articles or reviews.

Library of Congress Catalog Card Number: 91-65385

ISBN: 0-944072-17-8

Cover painting by Fairfield Porter
from the private collection of Roland F. Pease, Jr.
Copyright © 1991 by the estate of Fairfield Porter

FIRST EDITION
Printed in the United States of America

ACKNOWLEDGMENTS

The following editors accepted and published poems appearing in this book:

Clayton and Caryl Eshleman, *Sulfur*
Jim Hydock, *Brief*
Martha King, *GPWITD*
Askold Melynczuk, *Agni*
Joseph and Molly Torra, *lift*
Edward Foster, *Talisman*
Paul Hoover and Maxine Chernoff, *NAW*
Peter Gizzi and Connell McGrath, *o-blēk*
John Granger, *The Archive Newsletter*
Jake Kreilkamp and Jessica Moss, *Commonwealth School Literary Magazine*

Geoffrey Young's The Figures Press published twenty-one of these poems in slightly different form in the pamphlet *Remembrances*.

You would not be looking for me had you not already found me.

Pascal

CONTENTS

Beverly   3
Poem for Me Mother   4
Of Small Delights in Idleness   8
Tu Fu in English   9
My Grandfather Shovelled Snow   10
Melancholy   11
"Roast red hot pepper"   15
August Letter to a Friend   16
Landscape   18
"The stars are huge in the sky"   19
Hunter's Moon Birthday   20
"Assam tea tastes"   21
Morning Papers   22
The Earrings of Madame de —   23
Off 6th Avenue   24
Collarbone   25
On the Job   28
Bus Song   29
San Sano   31
To Rachel   32
J.R.   33
"This is the way"   35
West Concord   36
"Max wants out."   37
The Examining Room   38
Reading in Bed   39
Walk Across Boston   41

Expressing What is on my Mind   42
Passersby in Spring   43
The Painters   44
Early April   46
When I Read John Wieners's Selected Poems   47
Dejection   48
Jack Gilbert   49
Rossa Fortuna   50
A Shower in June   51
Not Even a Cup of Coffee   52
Twined Dreams   54
Lake Road   55
Lake Road Late August   60
Prose   64
Young Men Aging   65
Mother and Son   66
Out the Window   68
Drought   69
Trevor's Lake Ditty   70
The Kid With   71
In Fun   73
For Gerald Coble   74
Listening for Jane   75
Thanking Howard Norman for Paul Blackburn's *The Dissolving Fabric*   76
D-Day 1989   77
With John in Muncie   78

Peggy Gay   80
One Day   81
Bridgeport Station   82
Marni's Birthday   83
Labor Day   84
Home   85 ✷
In Passing   86
Masters of Wit, 1958   87
Joe Don Looney, R.I.P.   89
Reading C.K. Williams's "The Critic"   90
Hero   92
"Pardon, a few towns over,"   93
Damn Fool   94
Reading an Old Friend's New Poems   95
Before Christmas   97
Christmas Card   98
Lockerbie   99
Inside a Japanese Painting   100
Slipped twice and   101
Misremembered Edwin Denby Line   102
Jade Flower Palace   103
Late Winter   104
Snapshot   105
Playing Swallows Dare
Open Study Doors   106
Poem   107
February 29, 1988   108

For

Joe Brainard

Lee Harwood

John Yau

and

in memoriam

James Schuyler

1923–1991

BEVERLY

Dew like gray jade
cold as shaved ice.
Sun through morning fog
white coin on water
shaggy eminences emerge.
World, color of sage leaves.
These words for nothing,
breath on glass, but for you.

POEM FOR ME MOTHER

*Her title. I refused
her while she lived.
She fell down the stairs
dying far from me.*

Men cut the grass;
Jackie cleans house
vacuuming eight months
bugs off the carpet.
How full the lilac
and purple asparagus
slim in the colander
crumbs of dirt
on white stumps.
Unable to concentrate
on a page, not more
than a page and you,
no image yet you
in a dumb stare.
Yesterday at wind-eaten
dandelion skulls,
wind-driven seed everywhere.
Today skipping across
the mirror lake.
Flash of white hair
unkempt and noise of
panting shallow breaths
your last, your next to last
will the phone never ring
and find me folding
laundry or standing wet
freshly shaven.

Imageless? Images too.
The way you posed
for snapshots thrusting
forward from your waist,
modelling.
Once beside Easter forsythia.
See as clearly your face
collapsed in hurt.
You couldn't hide a thing.
And hear you:
"Why," you wanted an answer,
"are there so many ugly people?
Do they know?"

A boy cut your name
in his bicep, PATSY,
using a piece of slate.
Your father drove him away.
Teddy Perrone's hayrake
laying down a swath
carries across the lake.
Your father's daughter
no words of farewell.

We kept Duke,
our German shepherd,
down the cellar. He shit
in the crawl space,
his droppings aged
bearded and white.
Let's tell all our secrets.

Tell of Aunt Florence
favoring her relatives
and the money Uncle Al
promised in New York,
all our secrets again.

Utah: mall after mall
under mountains,
Orem cherries
and your ashes
dense, heavy grit
tinkle, just audible,
strike Timpanogos'
rockface.
Your things heaped
in boxes look like
they came from
the yard sale they
are on their way to.
They're not you
who squats to piss
cobble alley near
Vence's Hotel du Nord
Krug champagne drunk
at Pyramid Point fizzes
gold in the gutter
disappears in laughter.

Your force stopped
me cold, made me giddy,
monstrous I made myself,

cringed from touch and kiss
not to please you,
not to your face,
not until now.

    One Month Later

You're in your late thirties;
I'm a teenager. Dancing school:
blue suit, a pink shirt,
I remember, bow tie
and white glove resting
on her freckled shoulder
steering the blonde
then the tall brunette
with lipstick smeared gloves.
Miss Comer, Miss Waddel
on piano under your eyes.
Cold winter nights
the car heater warmed
a frost of ice inside
my window. You kept after me
to know everything.

Where pasture dips to woods
there is a rough pond
whose trees are gray sticks
and the bottom awful
unthinkable to touch.

OF SMALL DELIGHTS IN IDLENESS

Who is the Chinese poet
ancestor to me?
Who moored, drifts
behind backyard pigeon coop
choked by sumac where rats
fatten on white birds
until steel traps go off
like "dwarf artillery."
Beautiful phrase
remembered from James Joyce
set down this day in black ink.
Breeze that dries these words
shakes pink and crimson peony feathers.

TU FU IN ENGLISH

Do these poems remember
where they came from?
Like Rexroth, I too knew
Chinese poems in adolescence.
Pound's "Cathy" poems.
Got nowhere beating my brains
against *The Cantos* thinking
the pain must be good for me
and believing to admit
ignorance shamed me.
Better to lie
especially to myself
about what I love.
Then simply gave up
and turned the page
"While my hair was still cut
straight across my forehead"
and knew at once
if this is a poem
this is what I want to make.
And so I strive
weeding out my the's and that's
as I work troubled
by so many I's.
One day sure I have it
the next in despair.

MY GRANDFATHER SHOVELLED SNOW

from the witch hazel factory pond.
I see the scars skates made
and cracks packed with snow.
One day I will clear
hard ice for another's pleasure.
Old. I will be old,
he was, wear an overcoat
and shuffle not to fall.
There a boy bends
blowing over cold fingers
to lace tight his skates.
Alone since morning
he wakes from a nap.
Squabbling crows. A hammer
carries across the lake.
Push and lift new snow
white as this flowering peony.

MELANCHOLY

I meant to see
the swallows go
and mark their
going. Missed again.
The lines with bumps
are distant boats.
Late August wakes
a last few flies
to tread on me.
I could be a cow
slap and catch,
slap and miss
the slow washing
up to drill flies.
Unceasing crickets
hold my ear this
second with their
rachet, rachet.
Will the field
fill again with
grackles who hunt
and eat them?
The boys come, one
had his hair
parted by a crowbar,
to cut the lawn
once again letting
their mowers spew
grass on the walks
and driveway like
emptying the tub

leaving a green ring.
New mown grass
spiked with gasoline!
Your pink-purplish
lipstick traces
this glass as it
lipped the cup
I washed after
you drove home
in 5 a.m. dark.
I kissed the cup
closed the folding doors
built a fire
that put me to sleep
to wake stiff
alone, time my own
to eat if hungry
drink when dry
read through dinner
pouring another
glass of wine
washing down dessert,
a big chocolate bar.
A silver canoe
paddled by two
white shirts picks
off the sun's
declining light
shoots it back
hard and bright.
Jack paints his

roof with tar
to a licorice shine.
Thyme cut, bound
hung to dry.
Shell beans rot
short of ripeness.
Lunch's tomatoes left
a cold aftertaste
after-image of frosty
upstairs hallways.
Summer's last green
is gold. Fuzzy
goldenrod, sun faded
ferns into which
gold and rust
birch leaves fall.
Fishermen's voices
carry through morning
mist spilling up-
wards. Tomorrow
is today's soap, jam,
napkins, butter . . .
list to finish
cold drenched grass
sun scatters rhinestones
before a bath
noon stretches through
the door and lights
warm where standing naked
whiskers fall black
and gray on

bergs in water.
Details. Endless.
Single in attention.
All to see
and seen, register,
lose the world
in its details
one by one by one.

Roast red hot pepper
garlic, parsley, basil
ground to paste
smear on steaks
grilled over wood embers
corn on the cob
        many ears
and much wine
daughters Marni
        and Kate
since we drove west
all the way across
with your dogs
        Napo and Miss Bus
sip coffee then grappa's
green tint, fire
remembering some adventures
crunch of hailstones
outside Reliance
        forgetting most

AUGUST LETTER TO A FRIEND

Thunder from a distant corner
nods toward us as it passes.
Summer of mist and downpours
that lower feelings, cause
mind to rest on past events
and hurts yet to heal.
And so I write five months
and more since the night
you hurt and meant to hurt me
but then were surprised to hear
calls for an apology. You gave none.
(I think you damn well knew and
faked surprise, could not be called
to heed so great is your pride.)
We may be friends again but
is it to be polite, on tip-toe?
The rain recommences its delicate
march. What else is there to say?
Rain comes as it has come
all month from the south where
I imagine you will sit reading this
asking yourself what is it he wants?
For it not to have happened, first,
and for it to blow over as it will
but to sink in as well leaving
a small scar. A reminder that
my guard is up. You will not again
abuse this friend. Here, harder rain

trims red and violet anemone petals.
Anemos, Greek friend, your wind.
Do you know the Judy Holliday joke?
She enters a room, "Friend or anemone?"
Groan your groan. I've groaned mine.
I add her line because it came to me
as I worked delicately to unstick
the envelope that will carry this to you.

LANDSCAPE

Goldenrod at its height sways over browned clover. Thistle stalks shake loose stars of seed. Asters' skeletons though few lavender spokes linger. Where the last hay lays cut in bands crows settle on crickets. Broccoli yellowing to seed. Little for the bee. Feathery red poppies fall into gold umbrellas of dill. Lettuce raises towers many tiered and flounced. Pale grass and pink tipped grass. Crisp ferns. Sun roughens the sloping field. Fire through early frost.

"The stars are huge in the sky"
Hazy autumn. I gaze out
over the city. . . .
Not tonight. The Red Sox
open a three game series
with the Yankees in New York.
I watch TV.
This is the age of distractions.
In the city who ever
looks up? Stars are for
the country. Black nights
so amazing you wonder
where you've been.
We're no longer connected.
Powerful as we are
a thousand miles
is an instant.
Machines remember
and when we do
our childhoods come back
as anxiety.
The tune amid reeds
is lost on us.
Heard in words, yes
and seen in words
as the stars are huge
but lost in the living.

HUNTER'S MOON BIRTHDAY

     Bold sparrows seize crumbs.
Tea, watching
    people flow homeward
    my class soon to begin.
47   What to vow?
Give my all,
     everything, once
          and then
           once again

Assam tea tastes
like hay from
that May loft
we rolled down
a hill afterward
tipsy from beer
skipping school and
later spied Paul's
spinster aunt leave
the Loew's Poli
in mid-afternoon.
There's no light
little warmth this
morning no leaves
or few hanging
on after three
day's rain.
The sky is gristle.
Basil sorts among
ailanthus switches
and soggy leaves
lifts slightly his
puppy leg, pees.
We are worms
compared to stars
just finished reading.
Worms with noses
for fall's cold
rotten leaf and
earth smell.

MORNING PAPERS

    Eyebrow moon
canted, sets
as I rise to work
in other people's words
while around me
      lie books unread.
My pen digs
through the heap
and the morning passes.

THE EARRINGS OF MADAME DE —

Mist in St. James Street
pearl glow in Cambridge
tonight again Madame de —.
Mirror walls, white gloved servants,
champagne, smoke, carriages,
candlelight dances. All is whirl.
Suave Baron Donati, the diplomat.
A love story the first time
with what rapture they dance!
But Madame de — is silly, fainting
the Baron is nothing but charm
and her husband, the general,
what is it to be wise
in the way of her flirtations?
They are empty, Ophuls makes
us see, superfluous
going round and round
dinner with Henry Kissinger,
dancing at Palladium
and a cruise with the Buckley's,
Oscar de la Renta, Tina Chow,
Ralph Lauren, Bill Blass, Sister Parrish . . .
until they run down and die.
The Baron for honor. Madame de —
in a long swoon.
Those who ruled, pursued
as they were in pursuit
whose hearts were young
and beige.

OFF 6TH AVENUE

For Charles Simic

"Goin' out tonight?
Hey youuu . . . "
From . . . From where?
Above! High above.
Women prisoners
call through the bars
most of their words lost
and drop messages
on strings like spiders
to waiting pimps and lovers
who look heavenward.

COLLARBONE

Thrice broken right
clavicle pushed up
a calcium knob
forgotten until shaving
squinting catch in the
mirror its half buried
golf ball rise.
Broken first tackled
tumbling down
Stadler's yard em-
bankment. Six weeks
in a canvas sling.
Broken again playing
touch late afternoon
November 22, 1963
as I dropped back
to pass was hit,
blindsided and toppled
shoulder first
crumpled on hard ground
my collarbone
exploded.
The doctor waved
aside a break,
perhaps bewildered
to distraction as we were,
insisting my dangly
arm needed a wrench
back into its socket.
He had my friend
steady my other arm

then pull-twisted,
uselessly pushed
through my screams.
The doctor set
the shoulder under
a plaster yoke,
an armor cape,
a breast to beat
and make a hollow
noise.
Before I slept
drugged I drank
with friend Charlie
and Jack the bartender.
We saw ourselves
as we never were
unreal years before
hunched to Jack's radio
listening, acting
in an old movie.
I rode uptown through
stilled and grim
New York past mourners
coiled around Port Authority
like dark rope.
Ruby leapt in
the hospital waiting room
gunning Oswald down
then moments then
another doc cracked
and peeled

my plaster shell,
broke a third time
ill knit collar
bones to tie flat
ragged ends under
immobilizing strap.
It didn't work
and a bump rose.
Break it again,
they urged, one
hammer blow.
We'll put you out.
No. And today
I feel the lump
see a boy
who carried the ball
break his jaw
against a knee
that day, his tears . . .
we all saw tears.
We saw wet faces
we never expected to.
We innocents froze
in our tv's blue
haze four days
and slept off our
stupor in the dark.

ON THE JOB

Above Newbury Street
through the glare
dust in tiers
crippled Larry
chest pulled out of shape
right arm astray
he of the wife named Winona
recalls a train ride
holiday across Minnesota
the conductor calling out
"Next Stop Wee-Know-Knee!"
rousing me and Sandy Snowdale
(behind his door the boss
suffered through the "vapors")
from the afternoon's torpor
where I read
"the duplicate gray standard faces"
where I stole time
from work, from boredom
to write some first poems
words timid and plain
unlike Larry's cry
which has not left me.

BUS SONG

A Tuscan thorn
scratched the tiny
flap of leather
on this left shoe.
Good shoes. Under
them are loose stones,
oak leaves, dry
matted grass and
prickers bright
Christmas morning as
we carefully step
down to a stony
creek running beside
the white pebbled road.
No hunters. Very fine
young winter wheat
like green frost
in the furrows.
We are three
Marni, Nicola and me
who will feast on
goose, duck, risotto
finishing up with
a true plum pudding
hard sauce, coin
and all. Outside
persimmons hang rotting
from their tree.
San Sano . . . Attleboro
where trophies and

school rings are made.
Bonanza Bus. Soon
the Pawtucket spires
Providence in the distance
and through the copper
pineapple welcome arch
blowing on
my little horn
a Tuscan tune.

SAN SANO

Frost on tower window
up before the sun
burns it away
rubbed off
with nightshirt cuff
to look out over
rough smoking ochre hills
where hunters go
and in scrub oak
their guns pow-pow.
Tower brick are cold
quarter moon poised
above far hill's crest
halfway to Rome.
I am here to find
I miss my home;
that seeing is only
half done done alone.

TO RACHEL

My eyes liked to rest
on that blue flecked peagray
porcelain pot now smashed
after the kitten's clunky leap
brought a thick book down.
What can be kept?
Our New Year's Eve walk
that has left Umbrian clay
dried hard on my shoes?
Yes, and the gray fox
on a leash in Siena's Campio
Saint Stephen's Day —
if they persist into poetry
servant of memory.
Much else too,
more than I know
will return whole
one day, one day.

J.R.

For T.W.

Reflex. My hand
shoots up in hello.
His eyes turn away.
Son of a bitch!
I see my wave
plant its fist
in his pasty face.
Ten years friend
another ten enemy
and this wet day
your big head here
then passed like
a floury balloon.
No little whimpers
of regret. No
great lament for. . . .
For what? Cigarettes?
Beer? Loud opinions?
You cursing your
wife to shut up?
Friendship dead in you
in me dead but
the hurt burned
until that winter day,
rivers of rain
over rotting ice
and steam rising,
I slipped, thinking
on some stubborn
problem. Righting
myself I saw you,

saw you old man
as a good omen
here to remind me
how cold, how over
things can be
and still be in us.
I nearly slipped
again just now.
Back Bay Station's
slick marble floor
and high windows
steamed from rain.
Nothing to forget
nothing to forgive.

This is the way
the '90s begin
Monday, three days
after Groundhog Day
Martin Luther King's
shot dead again
then Bobby Kennedy, again.
On moonless, lightless
Roxbury Streets
kids murder kids,
above fortress stores
shots kill women
in armchairs,
a pregnant girl, strangled,
bludgeoned, dumped
doesn't make the news
where white men
plan Winterfest Boston.

WEST CONCORD

Better to hear
the jingle bells
sat up in bed
bells, yes, for real
bells coming near
sat up to look
down and spy
the horse from whose
halter rung bells
horse come slowly
out of snow's cloud
down the sidewalk
pulling a man tall
on his box plow
pulling him
into the blizzard
lost from sight

Max wants out.
Raise storm window
Christ, cold!
Saucer of moon
tips thin light
naked branches
shake, stop.
Must we be
what we do
do what we know?
Golden rooms
high up and
a block away.
Max wants in
pink meat cry
wants in *now*
wild green eyes
fur on end.
Arden's out there
and Beverly still.

THE EXAMINING ROOM

In socks and underwear
we're less flesh
than smells:
stink of stocking feet
and sweaty crotch.
A cheap Van Gogh print
looks down on this.
One of the pictures
he painted outside Arles,
every stroke obvious as counting.
There's a radio playing
where the aide
brings my vein to bulge
and draws blood.
Wouldn't you know
it's "Mr. Blue"
"headin' for the lights of town."
I left Mary blue
in her kneesocks
and Catholic school jumper,
and I can't forgive
irresistibly pushing away
Mary I kissed, swore I loved,
undid her clothes,
necked with until sore
and in bed alone
thought only of how
to free myself of her.

READING IN BED

Lulu playfully bites
my book-holding hand.
Tonight Montale's poems
"jubilee of birds."
Pigeons, Lulu's jubilee,
tantalize her from
the cornice above.
I look for poems
from his middle age
because I'm that old
myself and shamed
by youthful work
that reminds me
of what I did not do.
In a dark courtyard
Montale glimpses
a lemon tree
globes of yellow light
to thaw heart's ice.
Forsythia blazes here
and shivers. April's
breeze has its edge
clean and quick
to unmake any
presumptions of spring.
Lulu's at the open
window peering up
from the windowsill.
Another poem before sleep
to carry with me
to carry me away

as I was carried
as I want to be
by the stream at flood
breaking over,
smashing through
the swimming hole dam.
Swimming hole called
The Mines after
a cave where they
once quarried tungsten.
Dark mouth I
never went down.
The flood came at
the tail end of
a September hurricane.
You struggle to stay
above the brown floodwater
afraid of what rushes below.
Who knows what
is down there?
I think I did.
That's what scares me.

WALK ACROSS BOSTON

Fog around the Prudential's ears.
Rain intensifies oxblood
copper beech upper leaves
and wind turning garden trees
swell to a massy frieze.
Beers with Ray and talk
of Holocaust literature, *The Aeneid*
as "Beethoven played by Liberace,"
poetry bloodlines "You come to my
school and be my protege," Miles
Davis Birdland 1959 and glimpsed
crossing Madison Ave. sunglassed,
mint-green cream leather jumpsuit.
Walking home, rain now a spray,
passed the steep nosed balding man
seen here and there for years.
Full of whiskey brown Bass Ale
satisfied to walk off its slight
somber high and see fresh
in mind's eye Frank's photographs:
New Mexico highway as infinity,
coarse Butte, Montana curtained
smelterscape . . . in a dreamless daze
silver shrouded car, two palm trees
for bookends . . . Yesterday, these
tempted me from poetry.

EXPRESSING WHAT IS ON MY MIND

Up above and
across the way
masons point a house.
After work, rest but
so abrupt the shift
from class and students
I drink more wine
to slow myself down.
Soon to sojourn in hills
above lake. Mornings with book
and tea looking up to take it all in.
Steam rises off the lake
until it is nothing time and again.
Tapping of the mason's hammer
returns me to this end of the couch.

PASSERSBY IN SPRING

Oh, Louis Kesselman it's not you
walking, walking round Caspian Lake
lone tubercular Jew and not you
mad Cathleen of the wide brimmed hat
not Danielson in high topped shoes
who pass but ghosts newly housed
and strung round by lilac
overtopped with lavender lilac flowers.

THE PAINTERS

DeKooning, Jack "The Dripper,"
Guston, Kline *Life*
prints your paintings
Excavation, *Mahoning*,
Attar, *Blue Poles*,
compelling me to the cellar
where I brush housepaint
on woodscraps and shingles.
Dream of youth there to see
instantly ridiculous.
But the feeling, the freedom,
the charge in your work
is there to this day.
Bluhm, Goldberg, Hartigan,
Mitchell, Leslie, Held
book spread open on lap
how deep my pleasure
like swimming under water
not wanting to come up.
America accelerates so fast
the world we dream of living in
we grow up to discover is our past.
'50's world of us and them.
Painters celebrated for poverty
today celebrated for wealth.
Their New York a dream
ripening to a memory.
Mine, Blind Gary Davis
"Twelve gates to the city,"
Bob Dylan, astronaut splash
on TV in every store window,

crepe dressed JFK death
10th Street, The Cedar Bar
history. As quickly passed
New York of my youth.
Remember another "Life" photo:
Air Force officer Shoup used
to test G force, strapped
to a railway car and fired
like a bullet. A close up
of his wrenched and rubbery
painful grimace. We were all
in the future before we knew it.

EARLY APRIL

In Albert York's modest painting
"Skeleton with Nude in a Landscape"
death is faintly green echoing nature
but flesh is flesh, pink, foreign among trees.
How cherry pink are the petals
falling like ash over cigarette butts
as I write, my back to this tree,
New York already turning melancholy
with Marni's absence two months to come.

WHEN I READ JOHN WIENERS'S SELECTED POEMS

I look up from the book
read by sunlight. The wrong light.
Too stark. Not bright noon
but dawn after neon and moonglow.
My eyes smart. Huge trucks
shift gears down the avenue,
roar off with loads of rubble.
Sitting here holding my breath
murmur of traffic overtakes me.

DEJECTION

Failure the more failure
because April's light so crisp
limitless, abject in light
who sits writing this
under desk lamp's beam.
I took one further
step down toward
wampum and old gold,
toward bare corners
where the phone no longer
rings and people look
right through you.
Snow beclouds this
late April afternoon
a gust of paper
my twin fictions
flake and whirl.
I fear no deadly storm
I fear the light
I walk where I never belonged
scared, mind racing loss
no outward form to win.

JACK GILBERT

I thought names were coins
gratefully accepted anywhere.
I don't remember your reading
only afterwards in Dr. Watt's
living room asking you, severe face
constructed of sharp planes,
questions stitched together
of names: Lowell, Olson, Wilbur,
Ginsberg . . . I forget
what I wanted to know.
What I wanted was to impress.
This is one tough, cold spring.
A week before May it snowed
and the snow fell soft as shit on me.
Jack, I think I'm about
to put words in your mouth
but I also think together we're right
it is impossible to live
alone and afraid of life.

ROSSA FORTUNA

My errant hand
the broken cup
else Simmons might have me
teaching or home grading papers
another of the Collier brothers
instead I stop to sniff trees
clouds of cottage cheese turning
a little green.
My father was a glass blower
I don red underwear
for no one to see.

A SHOWER IN JUNE

Peeling a hard boiled egg
the downpour curls my hair
flick of shell into garbage can
where does memory not intrude?
Another June whose roses
swung "stitched and gored,"
the very words, across stone
swallows this rain and birds'
broken song. Memory
gorges every single thing
who are we to forget so much?

NOT EVEN A CUP OF COFFEE

So, none of us will go up
to offer the Choyo song
or any other. It is our fate
to suffer neglect, bitter
rivalry over small potatoes
and to bitch and moan
over this fate worse than death.
Imagine, brothers and sisters
if we were called how might
we answer and having answered
how might we be judged
by a huge audience caring
very much that our songs
live up to their wide
and close knowledge and high
expectations of what poems
must be. Imagine that we
are as scrutinized as
baseball players by crowds
who will not abide less
than one solid hit,
one good song in three.
We work our way up
through the minors
Pawtucket, Toledo, Albuquerque
writing songs to order.
Imagine, heroes to millions
our faces on poet cards
complete bibliography on flipside
and forgotten or disgraced
just as fast. Only so many

make the Hall of Fame.
So we curse our portion
our world squeezed
the shape of a lemon
hard and pitiless to the core
even as it leaves us free
to do as we damned well please.
But to be free where
so few care . . . what sufficiency
is there for us who mostly teach
others to pick up the same cares?
Tall and slender survive
birch trees hemmed close
by spruce and pine
far from the ballparks.

TWINED DREAMS

Eaves drip rain
beyond, unseen
a garden and uphill
fence wire holds pine
and chokecherry trash
short of hay before
open dark barn door.
Awake in this old dream
holding a gun up
another man's nose
until fear out bullies
him . . . I press a shot
through his head
making flesh cough.
No worse fear
than fear in sleep
that won't stay put
it wants another dream.
I know the man
rain erase his name
there's a crime in me.

LAKE ROAD

After work, a walk.
The morning rain
brought up sweet smells
and odors tempting
to Basil who, nose
high, goes after them
into the dandelions.
They come fast, go
as quickly to seed.
Few apple blossoms linger
white on a green bough.
The effect is Chinese
where a man's brains
squeeze out *ponk*
under a tank's tread,
where friend Katha is.
In our republic some leaders
are corrupt, others not.
A matter of character,
no standard to appeal to.
Our footsteps stop
a salamander. Alert, tense,
grayish-brown ridged back,
the color of dirt road,
but orange, lit from below,
bright, almost fake, orange.
Blackflies — worst
in thirty years — swarm
in a globe. They favor
ankles, wrists, ears. One

comes up my nose in a breath.
We can't stop too long
to watch the massed
creek water boil
where it comes out
under the road and pools
swirling, tea colored,
after rain on its way
to lose itself in the lake.
That strangled hooting
cry-laugh is one of three loons.
Uphill past fully fledged
arching out ferns
Holiday Home glumly
waits for renters.
No going down to Jane's
until after the 4th.
A big, slow white ruffed
part-collie barks and lurks
hunched over to sneak off
its own lawn and have a sniff
and Basil, being Basil and
a terrier, a growl.
I brought the leash.
Another slight rise,
another dog, large, cane-legged
a puppy the hair down whose
backbone stands on end.
He prances, bouncing
toward us. Basil stiffens,

snarls, teeth bared.
Back and forth, side
to side, the pup
doe-see-does his taunt.
There are more dogs
tied up behind this
house that holds
many sad marital tales.
Lupine, early, are out blue
and carmine pink, popsicles
above the scruffy field
running into woods
and curving down to Marga's.
There's a car. Workmen?
We won't visit again
that sunless, cramped house
instructions — stove, faucet, phone —
tacked everywhere, a riot of fuss.
Knee-high bluish haze
in the hollow where
a second creek plunges,
twisting white through
rain be-dropped ferns,
down making a swift noise.
Coppery golden birches
in twins and threes
limb-like trunks,
on her back
waving her legs,
are crusted with lichen
gray and gray-green

coppery too as they rise.
There's a photograph. Steiglitz's
Lake George black birches
cropped top and bottom
leafless, sexily entwined,
taken, perhaps, just before
he chased Georgia up the stairs.
This road climbs to
Campbell's Corners where
looking back the lake,
rough pines and boathouses
its edges, cuts an uncertain
shaped spilled mirror.
Calm after rain.
The old maples that shaded
a lawn, the house came down
for another's view, cleft
by lightning and age,
pull apart, a hiding place.
Downhill the road goes
to the stones where more sleep —
Sprague, Marga, Mrs. Perry —
every year who walked here.
We turn back encountering
both dogs who play as before,
pale worms drowned by rain,
sticky white bellied slugs,
but not one car.
Coming this way the lupine

field gives off an odor.
Something peppery, sharp. Celery?
Since the bottle bill
no beer cans, no six-pack covers.
Vermont can return
to its own state flower.
Which is?
We're up the long hill
and home, sweating as it
warmed as the walk warmed me
(Basil doesn't sweat
or do I remember he sweats
through his tongue?) and
scratching small bites red.
Home to *Nostromo*, wine,
a sausage and cottage cheese
dinner and too late for the country
but . . . basketball, Pistons vs. Lakers.
Civilization! Then up the brick
path, yellow pathlights overhead
to bed. Basil snores beside me.
Lulu curls into herself
at my feet. Moonless,
starred, black, a mask.

LAKE ROAD LATE AUGUST

In haze a walk.
The road scraped
ankle-turning rocks
turned up between
aisles of soft dirt.
We pass the berryless
blackberry canes.
Behind them goldenrod
grows into dusty pink
Joe Pye weed and above
these currents, asters,
lavender, newly arrive.
A car makes dust;
its driver wears a tie.
One week ago today
Bob Harney accepted
his new heart. Perfect fit
thought the doctors then
sudden, complete rejection
and quick death.
The creek is low.
We've had four days
total clarity, sky a dome
scribbled clouds its edges.
There's the ring of a phone.
 N — , he's renting there
near the lake through
those straight trimmed pines,
stopped by like an ancient mariner
to tell of his dead wife.
Her face, he described,

was black and then
his dog strangled
on its own chain.
Holiday Home stands mute,
empty save for two horses
grazing its brown pasture
who ignore us.
We'll go down to Jane's
Wednesday for dinner.
Fallen apples beyond her drive
crushed under grader's tread
smell sweet and Basil sniffs
but misses the wheel-crushed bird.
What a year for apples!
Rain, early and often,
plus sun enough has even
many suckered trees bent
low with reddening fruit.
From behind his hedge
Rudy creeps out,
gives Basil the once over
before his mistress calls him in.
The Gebbie Boys' truck
overfull with silage
slams past whipping up dust
to floppy leafed burdock
and singed, frost-curled ferns.
Purple crowns the thistle.
Mountains lost in haze
and the lake boatless

still, but in cricketness
we turn for home
kicking up a red shotgun shell.
Car from California.
Another from New Jersey.
Lupine looks like so many
burnt black baby fingers.
Overhead the sky is livid
and soon thunder's jagged grumble
with perhaps a drumroll of rain
or the delicate, wire brush kind.
Last night I thought
wine might slow tears
free my tongue and let
me say to the Harneys
what I felt and still
I blubbered and cried today
writing them all I could not say.
Just before dark we saw
the swallows are gone
yet paired hummingbirds
stay on drinking their fill
of sugar water to build
brown fat for the long flight
straight to Mexico.
We're in before the rain.
There's a book from Charlie.
Restovic's jubilant outhouse poems,
his world of devils
and golden beings

no more golden than Vermont's
last green gasp.
Basil snores at my feet.
Next week this time teaching.

PROSE

Our friendship has shrunk to postcards and jokes. You come east; I will be in the north. What is unsaid impossible to clear away. When we meet all talk will be of the old days.

YOUNG MEN AGING

Those days are so past
they never were. Something
else must have been happening.
Humor? Yes, and now jokes keep us
at arms length men who. . . .
What's the use? It was all talk.
Now talking from the heart
is done. If that's what it was.
Only it wasn't. We faked it.
What we wanted to say was
you're my friend; our friendship
will never end; I love you.
And not have to mean it.
Not have to mean more than
the desire to say the words
and the passion to inflect them.
Those desires answered the rest,
friend, is years that pass
cold into regretlessness.
Youth, ashes on the tongue.

MOTHER AND SON

Soiled milk smoke.
Green branches piled
on brush and set
afire in windless mist.
The man-boy lights
and guards it having
soaked his shirt
his shirt steams
as he piles higher
brush on flames
now visible snapping
up into bluer smoke.
He watches smoke
and fire. His mother
comes with a thin
bundle annoying him.
They quarrel, voices
cracking like fire
eating its way
through pine slash.
She hasn't minded
her manners he's
droning at her.
Practiced speech
steady predictable lash
rapture of bitterness
distilled, expressed.
He's pricked his
hand and cries out

then kisses the
thorn from his palm.
She's gone inside
out of the rain.

OUT THE WINDOW

After lunch I nap
sitting in a chair
and wake looking out
through the mess
of ailanthus branches
to lattice topped
decks until I stare
and all disappears.
I want to return
lean and wantless,
out from under
what crushes me,
but I never do.
What weighs
my heart is me.

DROUGHT

Hayed fields toasted:
corn seared ankle high.
Lakes fall, leave
a crusty pollen ring
baked on rocks
and boathouse walls.
Bugs hum in cedar shade.
Warm nights
after hot days
parch strawberries.
Streams barely water stones.
Dust pursues cars.

TREVOR'S LAKE DITTY

Dishes done
counter wiped clean
save the bump
of sticky stuff.
Pine sap?
With Kleenex
remove the bee
baffled by screen.
The dead thing
under the kitchen
turned out to be
a propane tank's
leaky spit valve.
Hop vines embrace
the tank with rough
wizard quick tendrils.
Pollen dust everywhere.
A fat crow shadow
creaks past croaking
belches, stuffed
with gore.
Ants patrol peony buds
bringing them to flower.
What for the ant?
Several postcards sent.
When southwind blows
clearing storms follow.

THE KID WITH

the slingshot
sings sweetly
as his younger
brother joins in
they walk the path
home after sniping
pebbles over water
at birds. Swallows.
Impossible to hit.
Ho hum, I wish I was
deep into, lost in
a thick novel
and not so easily
distracted by two kids,
the slight needle
of a grappa hangover
(my mouth tastes grass),
by thunderheads
several drops spotting
this dull book's pages.
I wish I was
a kid with a slingshot
walking Indian file
home leading his
sweet voiced brother
over pine needles
under dark pines.
I've just come
from the store,

two sticks of butter.
No one answers.
I last came through
this door the June day
school let out for summer.
I turn and
my brother's disappeared.
He left years ago.
There's change in my palm,
and a froth of dust
on the glass of milk
left out for me.
Mother, it's your son.

IN FUN

Under her helmet
of hair she sat
in the lifeguard's chair
bald as a marble.
It was in fun
I flicked her neck
like a bug and
in fun I caused
her wig to fly
off and slowly fall.
She blushed. She
cried. I saw what
in fun I came for,
her blue veined
barren skull. Below
the wig landed
in churned up sand.
There were others
I know who watched
her climb down
the lifeguard's tower.
They saw her bald-
ness same as me
who took the dare
who could not imagine
what she looked like
and was prepared
to lie the second
he saw and did.

FOR GERALD COBLE

The best hours
home from Paradise Point
are late Sunday
the house asleep
a thunderstorm upon us
cold thrill of air
dark rain, more wine
lights dance and die
and behind the rain
a deeper dark
it's a smell tonight
like cellar earth
a glimpse
of drama under torches
one of those days
we all have to
lie down and die
the rain in the wind
but not this day!

LISTENING FOR JANE

Hummingbird thrum . . . she's not there.
Whisk of leaf on shingled house side.
Motorboat and bee. A slow creak.
Screen door slam? No Jane.
Wind makes static in high grass,
raps on wood, wave against rock.
How deep the honeybee works
up creamy cornucopia-like flower.
They must be bells. Listening for
steps soft on old flagstones, sound-
less on lawn. Waves knock boats.
Unseen birds twitter lost in pine
boughs traffic. No Jane sound.
Mina, one eye pale blue, one green
speckled. Snowy Mina in among ferns.
Not by ear slow butterfly wings.
Strain to catch the home note
shushed in swimming kids laughter.
"Poor Sam Peabody, Poor Sam . . . "

THANKING HOWARD NORMAN FOR PAUL BLACKBURN'S **THE DISSOLVING FABRIC**

I heard Blackburn read once
1963 Lafayette College Easton, Pa.
Kelly and Rothenberg made three
down by bus from NYC $25 a man
and on to Allentown that night
reading next day at Muhlenburg.
There were twenty of us
and one member of the English
Dept. who put down the poets as
"Not my cup of tea, really."
      I can see Blackburn thin,
      sleek haired, goatee, raise
      his binder as a shield,
      tilt a pint of brandy
      to his lips and drink
      then stand to read.

D-DAY 1989

From sandy volcanoes
ants busily climb,
haze of blackflies,
solitary flying bug
and honeybee loud
as a purring cat.
So much life!
So far from
Tiananmen Square
where, the radio says,
soldiers strangled
dozens of protesters.
To wring a human neck
such intimacy and strain!
Do the hands ever forget?

WITH JOHN IN MUNCIE

When old
no mountains for us.
These fields and fields
and windbreak trees
will do.
Clouds come from nowhere
disappear two or three
days from here.
Indiana immensity
wastes desire, begs
comfort from common memories.
Again we stroll
beside the Po,
glimpse Turin's rhinoceros
come Sunday morning
Siena through Empoli
where the man drunk
before noon
was thrown from the station.
Through Pisa north
until poplar rows begin
and the highcheekboned
dark-rose hued beauty
boards laughing.
Has she become an old maid?
Not likely.
Did she marry a brute?
Die young?   No matter.
We talk her into life.
Hear the boys shout
playing basketball against

that barnside.
Her laughter
is as present, mouth
like a strung bow.
If we are dreaming
we have no need of waking.

PEGGY GAY

Up the escalator
in no weather, no landscape
but memory, she is Peggy Gay.
Her narrow breasts
softened by her sweater
buttoning up the back.
At the ballgame next day
same sweater, pointy breasts
get me, Peggy Gay.
Sweet breaking up inside
to let go and remember
Peggy Gay's French kiss
into mine, her breasts
against me and outside
beyond streetlight's shine
being allowed to caress
Peggy Gay.
Memory makes nothing
of thirty years.
Do I return to her arms
as she returns to mine?

ONE DAY

Giuffre's Fish Market's
been swallowed by
a hole in the ground.
Gone the rubber aproned men
who slapped fillets to paper.
Their fishman's scaly hands!
Through the tunnel under
the Southeast Expressway
above brick, above
the Custom's House pinnacle
shiny rose stone facades
boasting gold chevrons rise.
How long before their fall
and another's poems begins
So and So's Bank's
disappeared whole?
The only gain loss.

BRIDGEPORT STATION

Amtrak left the Bridgeport platform
a standing ruin, eyesore, home
still to a memory that yields,
seen from twenty years and countless
attitudes, yields nothing or refuses
anything more than a mustachioed bald man
shaking his son's hand and waving
his train away. The son then sees
two $20's in his unclasped hand
and below, through trestle timbers,
ridged grey water. Bridgeport harbor.
Again. Sees the gestures again. The end —
two who will never see
each other again- that will not end.
No martyred father, no martyr son
just the one turned to go and the other
sees him bald and black coated turn today.
So slip ties of blood. Let them go.

MARNI'S BIRTHDAY

Northwind blows glitter,
sunlight broken across
rugged gray lake water.
Cloud garment rent
blue peers through
years on the far side.
Twenty of these.
Bought a Bonnard book
to congratulate your mother,
welcome you.
My brother wrote: "Speechlessness."
Unprepared I had but
to be shown you
black haired, red faced
held in the nurse's arms
to put you in me.
Twenty years and ever
leaves here fall
on your birthday.
This wind blown noon
each rapid flutter
shakes itself in me.
I know it is you.

LABOR DAY

For teacher and student
the year begins when
leaves turn and fall.
Melancholy, weighing this,
sinking into memory
honey over ashes
my sightless stare
is broken by ducks.
Twelve, fift . . . no, eighteen
mergansers round
the glacial boulders
and steam off.
A few stand,
fanning wings outspread,
showing off.
Sun dries frost
and footprints disappear.
The fisherman hauls up
his spangled lure
shiny as no fish.
He'll leave then
I'll wade in naked
torturing myself
before the plunge.

HOME

Twenty-some years
not so long but
where you were raised
the ones who thought
you important are gone.
Druggist, mechanic,
lady from the beauty parlor . . .
no passersby know you.
Your house has known
two or three families,
been added onto, a dormer,
changed. The name you carved
on a windowsill, gone.
Sanded and painted over.
Street corners remember nothing
nor does the baseball field.
Not a tree or sidewalk
or cinder alley remembers.
That you cut yourself there
the ground has no blood
to remember.

IN PASSING

Below thin curtain
on front door glass
a cloud of fingerprints
anonymous as any breath.

MASTERS OF WIT, 1958

"Piggy" Lederer writhes
lashed by his rep tie
to a dining room pole.
After grace we sit
down to shepherd's pie
dry skin, gluey insides.
Someone has zits, headlights
we ooze shepherd's pie
between pursed lips;
Vesuvius erupts.
Dinner at the table
of Batman, spas math teacher,
and his silent wife
Maureen The Battress.
We begin with Clap Consomme.
The Bat forks up Mystery Meat
bright with oil
from the slicing machine.
Gonorrhea Gumbo? Lickety
Split Sauce? Topped off
with Syph Surprise after Bat
raffles the meat scraps.
The Battress looks down
at her clean plate.
She wolfed her food
like a stevedore.
One boy burps a sentence

complete with punctuation.
He gets his.
"Many friends! Oh,
lots of buddies. Legions!
Here's a dime
call your best friend.
Here's another dime
call 'em all."
Then finger his
wide lapeled sportsjacket.
"Nize material,"
a nasal Jewish tailor voice,
"such nize material"
causing him to stab
with a spoon. Paydirt!

JOE DON LOONEY, R.I.P.

Though far away, I see you still
run out of your cleats
from under your helmet
veer right, cut left, high step
Baltimore . . . Detroit . . . Washington
you made the papers today
long since you left
the Giant vets royally pissed.

READING C.K. WILLIAMS'S "THE CRITIC"

*"Blocks of cursive etched in softened paper, interspersed with real
  poems he's pasted in.
I hated to think of the volumes he'd violated to construct his opus,"*

I *like* to think of those volumes.
The world going about its business
not caring fuck-all for the poems
no matter their makers. No matter
the effort to select paper, correct
typeface, sew tight the signatures
and glue between boards stamped
with title and poet's proud name.
This reader may be a lunatic
but then Auden habitually cut poems
from books to paste together
his anthologies. Not that it matters.
This is the way poems live.
Think of the printer's errors. Think
of reader's memories that rewrite
lines to order then swear by them,
the wronger the more vehement.
Think of Sappho come down to us
because some Egyptian undertaker
wrapped a mummy in her poems.
Think of what goes on every day
in school. Even the hardiest poems
disappear into meaning under this
demanding scrutiny. Think of poets
appearing on stage to explain what
is on the page. Think of how
when the poem's written it's no
longer yours as if it never was,

as if it only stopped for a time
to be born and raised, or you tuned
in and this is what you received,
before it picked up and took off
for somewhere you'll never know.
Some bum with the heebie jeebies who
won't abide our conventions, who makes
a palimpsest . . . oh not so fancy . . .
a nest for the poems he's cut
like flesh from books and
returns to the scene of the crime.
Returns to let his scissors
thin books of poems and to write,
never giving those ravished books
a second thought, write his fill.

HERO

Miles. Birdland 1959. At first he wasn't there. Kelly, Cobb, Chambers, Cannonball. Chorus after chorus until he strolled on stage and turned his back to us. Jacket fit like a box. Soloing, he crouched into his horn then walked off on the applause. Turn blue. So cool we'd take his shit for a sacrament.

Pardon, a few towns over,
hating trade
        the touch of it
hung a money box
round his neck,
wore a pitchfork
for a hand.

DAMN FOOL

No luck in objects!
Neither Florentine wallet
nor coat pocket's
pound coin
        make
one good thing happen.

READING AN OLD FRIEND'S NEW POEMS

Twenty-one years
since we sipped
cheap bourbon
passing back
and forth
your poems
handwritten
on yellow paper.
November to May
friendship
tended a decade
and dropped.
Famous novelist
you travel.
Your new poems
cross rivers:
Brazil, Africa,
South of France
but forget
the Charles
we crossed
to drink more
and talk,
talk excitedly.
Is this what
makes me sour?
Sweet May
here again
friend
you hear
the loud

embraces of men,
boys really,
as we were then.
Or is it this?
Once we said
I love you.
Simple enough,
all men do.
Who cares to remember?
As with too much
the words served.
An age ago.
What, then?

BEFORE CHRISTMAS

Teaching done
    free mornings to come
full moon's
    tilted face
flattened, a little
slept on
    to one side
regards Boston's downtown
towers twenty-five years later
this bitter cold night
crossing the Mass. Ave. bridge
walking with Lee and Arden
down Cowbottom Hovel
    last year
it is always now,
    always then

CHRISTMAS CARD
IN MEMORY OF TED BERRIGAN
AND FOR MATTEO SPENDER

Seagulls on the athletic field
leafless rain wet trees
it's Mingus on piano
        "Oh *Lord* Jesus!"
Let there be money
enough for everyone
and Italia
Cortona-Orvieto-Roma
Bologna-Empoli-Torino-Torino
Florence rush hour racket
Fra Angelico monk cells
chaste, in perfect pitch
for me!

LOCKERBIE

Stoned on xanex
unable to fear flight
slowed like walking
        in sand
through dawn Brighton
I saw the headlines
bought the paper
hid it from sleepy Arden
who saw and hid
her fears for me
from me all the way
up to London
new passengers opening
their morning papers
replenishing a field
of infernos, fireballs, dead.
There won't, *can't*
be two Lockerbies . . .
They died so I might . . .
Nasty thought! Winked aside
through to Pisa
slept like a babe
on to Florence where
in great Santa Croce
I light candles
and in Orsanmichele's
        cave-dark
candles for these
so many more nameless
innocents unaware
blown out of this light.

INSIDE A JAPANESE PAINTING

For B.K.

How close sleep
is to new snow
and so we walk
(we almost stroll)
where the peonies
flourish in memory only
and ice sleeves
the cherry boughs.
Our shoulders brush
we giggle, whispering.
There, peony stalks
scribble.
We are inside
a pearl, nothing
between us and snow
but your umbrella,
snow covered,
a roof as we go.

SLIPPED TWICE AND

nearly fell coming home
even taking baby steps
so slick the sidewalks
last night's rain iced over.
We were in before the freeze
walking through steam
from snowbanks steaming
under warm misty rain
and the streets aslime
with icy grit.
O, youth and thrilling
crystal aftermath
ice storm's morning
glitter and creaking
branches ensleeved,
bowed back trees,
sheared off limbs
and spinning wheels
razory whine.

MISREMEMBERED EDWIN DENBY LINE

Basil's turd steams
           rutted dirt
crinkly pane of puddle ice.
A passing jet leaves
silence in its wake
four or four-thirty
           Monday
think what's on our plate!
           Gutters
adrift in winter dreck.
A waste river,
           random-
ness that is
the more perfect order.
Plastic bag flaps
           treetop high
our flag still . . .
           "Happiness
in a world of shit."

JADE FLOWER PALACE

There are no ruins.
What was must be
a world conceived
in memory alone.
It's not that the bearded
lady and all her
wino boarders are dust.
Walking these streets
you cannot believe
they existed. It is the will
to annihilate the past,
to wipe clean and begin
again from the ground up,
the past so much filth
to be carted away.
If you point and say
this was where . . .
who will believe you
faced with upright acres
of concrete and glass so new
no past can be imagined?
Time is not the enemy.
Where men turn their backs
who can say what
the years have lost?

LATE WINTER

It's snow I love
heavy on spruce boughs,
making slush in gutters,
icicles from eaves
as when we first came
and does today.
Big fluffy flakes.
It's lights on early
against afternoon dark,
smoke in bars
where friends meet
even though the bar's closed
and friends have disappeared
with the years.

SNAPSHOT

Image from the angelic '50s
caught by Robert Frank
caption by Jack Kerouac.
Black man snores
head in white drunk's lap
whose arm caresses, guards him.
Sure, they may beat each other
to bloody mess by nightfall
or morning but in these days
when success is again style
their tenderness is not amiss.
And yes this romanticizes
those years of my youth
and heroes Pollock and Parker
their brilliant damage.

PLAYING SWALLOWS DARE OPEN STUDY DOORS

whip in,
corkscrew up
eaves height.
No exit.
Fainter
their flutter
some light
on rafters,
shit,
as this one
jerks thrice
its tail
winding up
and Zap
down
stops, one,
two beats,
suave gesture,
Ready
he throws
himself straight
through doors'
wall of light
veers up
peach under
blue flare
bright, free
chattering
to his buddies

POEM

London Perceived
placed just so
weeks ago to fall
into the water bucket,
falls. Fate.
Its pages stick. Ruined,
the book goes out
with the trash cursed
by the clumsy hand
that bought it twenty-
five and more years ago
in Bridgeport, The Open Book,
on the way to Rhode Island
where we snuck out late
to make unmarried love,
mostly clothed, beneath
a backyard tree
that tonight we may
ride pleasure harder
no tippytoes, bed not grass,
no old woman's woken
cry in our dark house.

FEBRUARY 29, 1988

To Hendrick Avercamp, mute
to Jim Woods coal-rattle
voice of the 1975 Red Sox
and to Dick Albert, weather oracle
whose birthday this is
this poem that remembers another
poem eight years ago to the day
walking across Boston in zero
cold, remembers but will not be
of now and then on this day
of four years in one.
When we enter the past
it is into a world of our own:
the future is ours in common.
Today is sunny, mild.
Green spears of some plant
plunge through backyard gravel.
Workmen labor coatless.
Everything that gives order
to our lives, that we do
over and over again
abandons us or we must
abandon it. We cannot resist
the drive towards disintegration.
Ignorant as we are we
can be assured of this.
Sweet natured Frank, Mauch Chunk lad,
fell and cracked his skull
going in to see "The Dead"
and now is dead himself

under the falling snow
never having regained a
particle of his civilized mind.
He follows Marga who went fast
at the end. The scythe will soon
lay low all that generation.
All those we meant
to charm and impress, be
accepted by as well as all
we mocked with nicknames,
turned away from; all who gave
our youth shape die as we were
told they would. Suddenly
your halfway up, halfway
there is halfway down
the less crowded stairs.
Your arrow flies on its way
the only defense, defenselessness.
Frank, Marga they are in us
as we will be in those
who come after. Jim Wood's voice
speaks through another rain delay
of the Crackers and The Golden
Greek from Birmingham. Avercamp's
pantalooned skaters, lace collared,
flirting, whack golf balls on
ice hard as rock under them.
These we value. The one dis-
appears into summer air
as he fills out summer's dream;
the other sharpens winter's brilliant

edge, winter's social promise.
And Albert cracks our future like a code
or nut with daffy joy that
tomorrow's weather is his, *his*
storm to come that breaks records
set in March of 1978!
Down comes the scaffolding, nerve
structure in place and facade
set by twenty years' practice
(You *know* you are not the fraud
you feared you were) when
in sneaks a worm. As you
wanted to be so you have
become. You rehearsed funeral
speeches and now you have given
them, spoken over father-in-law
Sprague and friend Marga in one year.
Melancholy, sick tooth of life,
your tongue returns to it
sweet thrill of pain! Not grief.
Unseemly to grieve for the long-lived.
It is the blues, slow increment,
sadness alongside certainty
that it has come down to you
as it had to. For a short time.
In America everything takes longer
to happen. We have stretched out time.
You can be seventy and still
the daughter of your mother who
repeats her story of your father

courting her on horseback.
Then, dear Jane, she dies and her
hundred years is an instant.
Nothing stands still and anything
will happen. It is a fallen world
and impossible not to rise,
not to renew itself. Is the curse
not ending but the endless
beginning again? The crocus persists.
Birds return to the steel girders
of an overpass. Tulips and daffodils
draw bees in February as March
gathers speed over Canadian prairies
and issues bold southern disclosures.
Tomorrow the highs and lows
will make no lion. Daylight lengthens
no matter how many raw lambless
days there are to come. It is good
to be home before dark
a breath of clean smelling
soon March air in the street,
to love another as a restless
boy could not and hear the sound
she alone makes opening the door,
to respond to the calls of your children
as they grow into their own lives,
to love friends beyond judgement,
to pour wine, to see plain
that none of this is all there is
and to have the memories
of those gone before to serve.

ABOUT THE AUTHOR

William Corbett lives in Boston and teaches at Harvard Extension and Commonwealth School. Zoland Books published his book of poems, *On Blue Note*, in 1989.